How to PAINT on FABRIC

Freehand, Tracing, Stamping, and Stencil Methods for Beginner and Advanced Craftsman

by Marge Wing
with N. Mahr, L. Young, and G. G. Grimshaw

CROWN PUBLISHERS, INC., NEW YORK

**Dedicated to
Artist Margaret Pfeiffer Endter, our mother,
who with her great love inspired
and taught us how to paint and create**

Inquiries should be addressed to Crown Publishers, Inc.,
One Park Avenue, New York, N.Y. 10016.

Printed in the United States of America
Published simultaneously in Canada by
General Publishing Company Limited

LIBRARY OF CONGRESS CATALOGING IN PUBLICATION DATA

Wing, Marge.
  How to paint on fabric.

  Includes index.
  1. Textile painting. I. Title.
TT851.W56 1976   746.6   76-27883
ISBN 0-517-52663-8
ISBN 0-517-52664-6 pbk.

Designed by Laurie Zuckerman

Contents

Acknowledgments

We wish to extend our sincere thanks to authors Carla and John Kenny, for without their encouragement and help this book might never have been published.

We gratefully appreciate the cooperation of Alice John Rogers for the many fine clothes she loaned us from her store.

To Bennett Yell, the photographer, admiring and respecting his talent and fine work, we shall always be very thankful.

To Catherine Murray our sincere gratitude for her perfection in typing the manuscript and always being so willing to be of assistance.

To Grace and Severen Loeffler we express our sincere thanks for their interest and help in the early stages of this book.

To Edith McCowan of Schramm Galleries a thank-you for her help and enthusiasm.

Many thanks to the models for their patience—Patty Anderson, Janie Malin, Joan Yell, Ann Wier, and Marguerite Swigler.

All photographs by Marge Wing unless otherwise credited.

Preface

Now, you can handpaint exciting and personalized clothes, you can handpaint handbags, scarves, shoes, and many other accessories to enhance your wardrobe, and you can handpaint all kinds of special home furnishings. The numerous photographs will show that there is no limit to the various objects it is possible for you to paint. We want to inspire and encourage you to create and develop your own ideas, and you can, by following the instructions and the step-by-step illustrations. Let us impress upon you that this is not a complicated or involved technique. The combination of paints that we shall show you how to use are just brushed on, allowed to dry overnight, and that is all there is to it. No before or after treatment is necessary.

Handpainting on fabrics is a very old art form and can be traced back many years to the Chinese who painted on silk and other fabrics. It is interesting to know that Martha Washington wore a handpainted dress of "salmon pink faille with a design of wild flowers and insects of North America in natural colors." This is a quotation from a book on all the First Ladies by G. Z. Brooks. Today, handpainted clothes are being shown in this country and Europe by some of the best fashion designers.

Over fifty years ago, artist Margaret Pfeiffer Endter experimented with paints on fabric and created a combination of paints which proved to be workable, washable, and dry-cleanable. We, her daughters, continued to use and perfect this technique to the point where we were able to paint on any fabric in any color. The proven durability of our painted items, which is one of this craft's most important aspects, made it possible for us to paint clothing, items for the home, and fashion accessories, and sell them to fine stores all over this country.

Foreword

To Marge Wing, fabric represents living canvas. And to the many women who have collected her handpainted fashions and accessories, she is an artist of unique ability. In this delightful book, Ms. Wing shares her creativity with all of us, in the same expressive manner she applies paint to fabric.

In her own words, "We feel that a book on this subject can be important, not only in the field of crafts, but as a commercial opportunity for a person after learning our technique." Here is an art form, ages old, that is tremendously exciting in its new applications. Through a long and very successful relationship with Ms. Wing, we have greeted her fans with an ever-changing palette of handpainted fashions. Now she inspires all of us to take brush in hand and apply our own talents with her know-how. We learn all there is to know about handpainting from preparation of fabric to application of the paints to clothing, accessories, and items for the home. Through a wonderful variety of illustrations, the instructions become beautifully clear.

At a time when handpainted fabrics are an important fashion trend both here and in Europe, *How to Paint on Fabric* is a vital new book for an aspiring artist to own.

EDWARD BONNEAU
Saks Fifth Avenue
Fort Lauderdale, Florida

1 Introduction to Handpainting on Fabric

If you are an amateur or professional, young or old, you can learn to paint on fabric by following the instructions in this book.

As you read through this book and look at the many photographs of what it is possible for you to accomplish by learning to paint on fabric, be conscious of the opportunities being presented to you to be commercially involved by creating something salable. One of the most thrilling experiences you will ever have is when you have painted something of your own creation and someone says, "I'd like to buy it!" The possibilities of your being inspired to create new and exciting forms of art to be merchandised have not been dreamed of yet, but through your own initiative and effort you can open many doors to work that will keep you happy all your life. We sincerely hope this book will inspire you to try.

Handpainting on fabric as a hobby can be very satisfying, and like other handicrafts it can be of great value to many charitable organizations which depend on craft artisans to donate their work for moneymaking projects. We suggest that giving of your talent always be considered.

Our technique of painting designs and various subjects on fabric has been used by us commercially for more than twenty-five years. Fabric thus painted has proved to be hand-washable and dry-cleanable and will last for many years when taken care of properly. Currently, clothing in all categories—sports, casual wear, and evening clothes—is being handpainted and shown by top designers in fine stores everywhere.

Some of the many other items that can be attractively painted are: pillows, lampshades, bedspreads, draperies, fabric-covered wastebaskets, mat sets, guest towels, luncheon sets, fabric and suede shoes, lingerie, handbags, and hats. Photographs of some of these are shown throughout this book.

In the following chapters we shall give you all the necessary information, plus illustrations of the technique we have perfected, so that you can quickly master the use of the paints and create whatever you want.

Materials Required

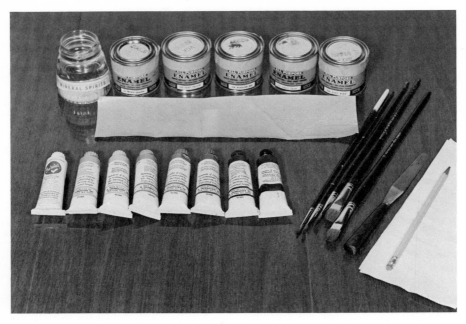

Materials required—high-gloss enamels, artists' oil tube paints, mineral spirits, artists' flat sable brushes, palette knife, types of paper.

Five ½ or ¼ pints of oil-base high-gloss enamel
   Colors: white, black, yellow, green, red
Artists' oil tube paints
   Colors: titanium or zinc white, lemon yellow, cadmium yellow light, cadmium yellow orange, alizarin crimson, Harrison red, geranium lake, Prussian blue, mauve (true purple)
Artists' flat sable brushes (long handled)
   Assortment of sizes and at least one small pointed brush
Mineral spirits
Palette knife
Notebook paper or typing paper
Tracing paper and stencil paper called Vellum, which is transparent
Graph paper

The high-gloss enamels come in various shades of the colors listed. When choosing them, use the color chart that paint stores supply and get the brightest yellow, a strong green (fairly dark, as it can always be lightened), and the red should be the most brilliant true red.

The high-gloss enamel (best quality) and mineral spirits are available in any paint store. The artists' oil tube paints listed are the colors you will need, but there is a very wide range of colors available if you want to experiment with them. These oil tube paints, brushes, palette knife, tracing and Vellum paper are found at any artists' supply store.

Investment in these supplies will enable you to paint many, many items, as the amount used on any article is minimal.

Choosing Your Fabric

Practically every type of fabric is paintable—light or dark, thick or thin, smooth or textured. The new synthetics such as polyester, antron, nylon acetate, and so on present no problem. All the standard fabrics such as cotton, silk, chiffon, taffeta, felt, suede, monk's cloth, burlap, canvas, denim, and smooth knits have been successfully painted by us for many years. With this wide range of fabrics to choose from, we suggest that you avoid such fabrics as fuzzy wools, terry cloth, bulky or loosely woven knits, as you will not be pleased with the result.

Fabrics should always be smooth, with no wrinkles; iron if necessary before painting. When the painted fabric is allowed to dry completely overnight, it is hand-washable and dry-cleanable. If the fabric is washable, use soap that is correct for the fabric, and the painted design will wash successfully. If the fabric needs pressing, iron the painted area on the back. If the fabric can be dry-cleaned only, a good dry cleaner can successfully clean it. For more than twenty-five years we have proved these statements to be true.

Consider handpainted fabric like any other fine handwork (such as hand-done embroidery, needlepoint, crewel, or lace) as delicate, and it should not be included in the family wash. It should be hand-washed for long-lasting results.

It has been proved that letting fabric drip dry, whether it is that type or not, is more satisfactory than squeezing and wringing. Very tight wringing is detrimental to any fine handwork.

Preparing Paints and Fabrics for Painting

Place the cans of enamel within easy reach, as with your brush you will dip right out of the cans. Stir them well each time they are used, especially when first opened. Place a piece of foil paper or contact paper approximately 12″ × 5″ in front of the cans for your oil tube paints. Squeeze out not more than one-half inch of the oil tube paint colors you will use for your design on the foil or contact paper. These oils will remain usable there for a long time. Place a piece of notebook paper or typing paper in front of the oils to use as your palette for mixing the paints. A few pieces of Scotch tape will hold it in place so that it doesn't slip while you are mixing your paint on it. Place a small glass jar of mineral spirits beside the enamels. This is for thinning your paint and cleaning your brushes. This convenient arrangement of your paints and brushes is shown in the photograph.

On your palette squeeze out white oil tube paint and with your palette knife dip out an equal amount of white enamel (or measure one teaspoonful of each at first until you become familiar with its consistency) and mix with your palette knife on your palette until it is a smooth consistency, as shown in the photograph. Keep this mixture on a corner of your palette, as you will need it all during your painting. We shall refer to it in the instructions as "heavy white."

Place a piece of smooth paper under the fabric you are going to paint so that the paint that soaks through will be caught by the paper. Under the paper place a piece of cardboard so that you can pin down the fabric all around the area you are going to paint. This is necessary in order to keep your fabric stretched out and smooth, otherwise your brushstrokes may pull it.

Stretchy fabrics like chiffon and sheer jerseys paint well, but due to the delicacy of the fabric they have to be pinned down on the paper and cardboard every few inches around the area you intend to paint.

Place cardboard in between the front and back of a jacket. Next, paper is placed on top of the cardboard to catch the paint that soaks through. The cardboard makes it possible to pin down the fabric and hold it in place so that it won't slip while you are painting.

Cut cardboard to fit in pant legs for the same reason.

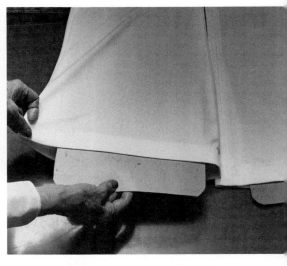

Placement of paints within easy reach, and the mixing of the white oil paint and white enamel with palette knife to make "heavy white." This "heavy white" is a very important paint mixture and should be done before you start to paint.

2 Painting Techniques

Painting on fabric is like painting on any other surface except that the paint soaks into the fabric. When the paint soaks into white or pastel-colored fabric, the color of the paint you are using is barely affected by the color of the fabric. But when you are painting on dark or brilliant colors the paint will change according to the color of the fabric.

Smooth fabric is easier to paint on; however, rough or textured fabrics can be very effective and often lend an interesting background. If your design is going to be intricate and finely detailed, it is better to put it on a smooth fabric. But when you are planning a large splashy design you can put it on any texture. You will learn and understand this easily by experimenting on various fabrics. Practice on scraps of all types of fabric first in order to get the feel of the paint and become familiar with its application and reaction on various fabrics. Also, this will give you the opportunity to learn to mix the enamels with the oil tube paints to get the colors you want. Don't start painting on dark or brilliant fabric until you feel confident in the use of the paints on white or pastel fabric. The process of overcoming this is explained in this chapter.

The combination of the enamel, oil tube paints, and mineral spirits is the basis of our technique. The oil tube paints are used strictly for color and must *always* be mixed with the enamels. With your brush you will always mix the colors you want on your paper palette. You can paint with just the enamel, since it is the basis for its permanency, but *not* with just the oil tube paints. Oil tube paints by themselves will not wash or dry-clean. The enamels are all basic colors, but by mixing them with the oil tube paints you can arrive at any color in the rainbow.

As an example, to paint a pink flower, put several brushfuls of white enamel on your palette and add a touch of red oil tube paint. Mix until you get the shade of pink you want. Or, to paint a yellow flower, use the yellow enamel and either add yellow oil tube paint to make it more brilliant or add white enamel to make it a pale yellow. Practicing mixing paints to arrive at the color you need is a very instructive experience.

Your first coat of paint on the fabric will be a thin coat and you will brush in the complete object with the color you have mixed, which includes the enamel, oil tube paint, and mineral spirits. Test this on scraps of your fabric to see if it will spread and cover smoothly; if not, add more mineral spirits.

This first coat makes a wet base for dark shading, finishing light touches, and fine details. Try to keep from overpainting your design with many coats. The object is to avoid a big buildup of paint, as it will make your finished product very stiff. This is very undesirable on any fabric.

The "heavy white" is one of your most usable combinations of paint. It is the basis for all your highlighting—for instance, in edging the sails of a sailboat to show how they curve into the wind. Use it in green enamel to make the highlights on a shiny leaf. Use it with a little pink oil tube paint to accent the most prominent petals on a pink rose. In the step-by-step illustrations in this chapter you will see this explained.

In chapter 5, Patterns, many sketches of designs are shown to help you. In addition, information is given as to where to find pictures of subjects you want to paint.

Freehand Painting

Painting freehand with a brush has advantages over using stencils, a tracing, or stamping method. It is quicker and has a freer and more spontaneous look. Don't be hesitant in trying it even though you make mistakes, as it will give you confidence in controlling the paint on your brush. Practice on scraps of fabric—the more you paint the more quickly you learn.

The following illustrations and step-by-step instructions show how to paint sunflowers. They have a large brown center with light prominent seeds, and the petals are a brilliant yellow and orange, uneven in size and floppy rather than stiff. Plan the size and placement before you start painting. Prepare your paints as described in chapter 1.

On your paper palette mix red and green enamel and a little mineral spirits to make a deep brown. With your brush mix yellow enamel with some of this dark brown to make a lighter brown. Then paint a circle for the center of the flower and an oval, leaving the top half of the oval open for petals.

With the light brown mixture fill in the circle and the oval. Pick up some of the dark brown paint on one corner of your brush and paint the uneven edges of the circle and the lower part of the oval. Then paint a dark circle in the center of each.

Mix yellow enamel and cadmium yellow oil tube paint with mineral spirits to make a bright yellow. Paint the petals, making some of them longer than others and some overlapping one another. The lower flower, being partially turned over, shows petals falling over the center.

With the bright yellow you have mixed, fill in all the petals. If your paint doesn't spread easily, add more mineral spirits.

Mix yellow enamel with cadmium yellow and orange oil tube paint and mineral spirits to make a deep orange. Pick up some of this color on the corner of your brush and start brushing from the center out. Paint some of the petals a deeper color to show that they are behind others, which makes the top petals stand out. Some petals will show only partially, while others will show completely. All of this is accomplished with your deeper shading.

Mix green and yellow enamel and mineral spirits and paint the leaves and stems.

Mix green enamel with a little black enamel and a little cadmium orange oil tube paint to make a deep olive green. Pick this up on a corner of your brush and paint the edges and veins of the leaves. Also darken the stems and little green leaves on the turned-over flower.

Mix "heavy white" with yellow and orange oil tube paint. Pick it up on the corner of your brush and edge the petals with it, accenting those that are on top of others. This use of "heavy white" is explained in detail in chapter 2, Painting on Dark and Brilliant Fabric.

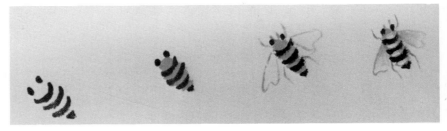

At the top of this painting you will see how to paint a bumblebee freehand. With your pointed brush and black enamel, paint two eyes and three curved black lines plus a little tail. With the bright yellow paint you have mixed, fill in the spaces in between. Mix a little white enamel in the black enamel to make gray and faintly outline wings and legs. Since the wings are transparent, mix white enamel with a touch of blue oil tube paint to make a pale blue and paint them a very light color.

Mix "heavy white" with yellow oil tube paint and paint seeds around the center of each flower. Using some of this mixture in the green you have on your palette, you can accent the leaves here and there to make highlights.

Practice doing freehand sketches in pencil of anything and everything. Doing this often trains your eye to see things in perspective and gives you confidence to look at something and be able to sketch or paint it to your satisfaction. Give thought and planning to your idea before you start. Using a brush and paint to sketch in your subject will be easier if you have done a lot of pencil sketching.

Watermelons were in season when this was painted, and studying them in the market, where there were whole ones and quarters, you realize that each one has different markings running along it from one end to the other. The slices were all a beautiful coral color in the center with darker red indentations where the seeds were. Watermelons make a colorful addition to any arrangement of fruit or as a special design for a casual skirt, as shown in one of the photographs.

Following is a step-by-step instruction of a very easy arrangement of watermelon.

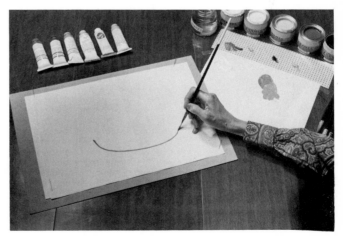

1. Prepare your paints for painting as described in chapter 1. Pin down your fabric on a clean piece of smooth paper, such as typing paper or notebook paper, which has a piece of cardboard under it. This keeps the fabric from slipping and the paper underneath catches the paint that soaks through.
2. On your paper palette mix green enamel with yellow oil tube paint and mineral spirits and paint half of an oval to make the bottom edge of the slice.

3. Mix white enamel with a little red oil tube paint to make a coral color—a touch of orange oil tube paint may have to be added—and paint a straight line from one end to the other of the half oval slice.

4. With the same mixture of green enamel, yellow oil tube paint, and mineral spirits, paint an elongated, oval-shaped, whole melon behind the slice, using a fairly large brush.

5. Mix "heavy white" and yellow oil tube paint with a little mineral spirits and paint the markings on the skin of the watermelon behind the slice, going from one end to the other following the curve of it.

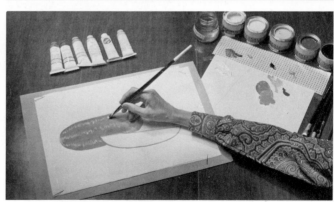

6. Mix white enamel, a little yellow oil tube paint, and a little green enamel with mineral spirits and paint a strip of this color just above the green outline of the slice.

7. Using the same coral mixture you have on your palette, paint in the complete upper half of the slice.

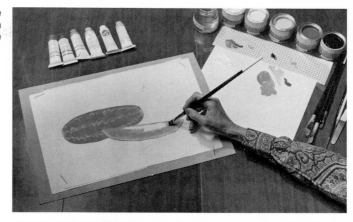

8. Mix red enamel with a little alizarin crimson oil tube paint on your palette and pick it up on one corner of your brush, in order to have control of it, and paint indentations around the lower half of the slice where the seeds are.

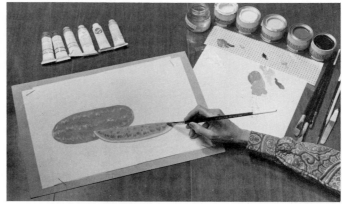

9. With black enamel right out of the can (add no mineral spirits in order to keep it concentrated), paint in the seeds.

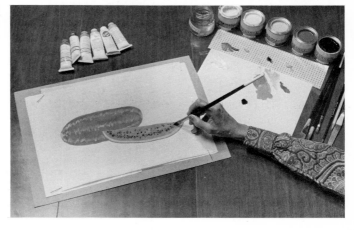

The Tracing Method

Tracing can be done only on fabric thin enough to see through; otherwise use the stencil or stamped-on methods explained later.

When painting on thin fabric, the paint spreads very quickly, due to the fact that the thinness of the fabric allows the paint to soak through rapidly, with a lot of the paint going through onto the paper underneath. Very little paint is absorbed by certain fabrics such as organdy, chiffon, and other similar fabrics. Test your paint on scraps of the fabric you are using to get the right consistency. Mineral spirits should always be mixed with the enamel on your palette, as it is too thick to use right out of the can. Don't have your brush full of paint when you start to brush it on, as you can't control it if it starts to spread beyond your design. Start out by picking up a small amount of the paint on your palette with your brush until you become familiar with the reaction on the fabric.

Tracing is the simplest of all methods, but you will have to learn the other methods in order not to restrict yourself from painting on all types of fabric.

The following step-by-step instructions and photographs concern coral-colored hibiscus with buds and leaves. This same procedure should be followed with any other design. Prepare your paints as explained in chapter 1.

1. Make a heavily outlined drawing of the design.

2. Place the drawing under the fabric, which has been placed on a piece of white paper and cardboard, and pin down at each corner. With a pencil lightly trace the design through on the fabric. Remove the drawing and proceed to mix on your palette white enamel, mineral spirits, and a little red oil tube paint to make a coral color and brush in the whole flower and the buds.

3. Mix red enamel with alizarin crimson oil tube paint and darken the centers of the flowers and stroke it up into the petals. Mix on your palette green and yellow enamel with a little yellow oil tube paint and mineral spirits to make a soft green and fill in the leaves and stems.

4. Add more green enamel and a little black enamel to the green mixture on your palette and darken the edges of the leaves and the veins.

5. Mix "heavy white" with a little red oil tube paint to make a soft pink and lighten all the edges of the petals. Mix red and green enamel with a little yellow oil tube paint to make a light brown and paint in the stamens. Mix "heavy white" with a little yellow oil tube paint and dot on the little seeds. Add "heavy white" to the green paint you mixed for the leaves and highlight the leaves to show that they are rippled rather than smooth.

Remove paper underneath and replace with clean paper and allow to dry overnight.

The Stamping Method

For thick, thin, or dark fabric a stamped-on method can be used. Draw or trace your design *heavily* on tracing paper, turn it over and on the back, with your pointed brush, carefully outline the design with "heavy white" or any other color you want with "heavy white" mixed in it. Then stamp it on the fabric, pressing down with your fingers. The reason for "heavy white" in the color paint you want to use is that it keeps the outline from drying before you finish it. The only exception is if you want to stamp on something in black, use the black enamel right out of the can, as it will come off readily on the fabric. This method works successfully on any fabric except *extremely* rough textured fabric, in which case the stencil method should be used.

Practice this stamping method on scraps of fabric until you become familiar with it, as we use this method more than any of the others because it has proved to be the most workable for most designs.

The following step-by-step instructions and photographs explain this method. Prepare your paints as explained in chapter 1.

1. Have your fabric ready and pinned down to a piece of paper with cardboard under it. With pencil and tracing paper make the outline of a butterfly. Using a pointed brush, outline the butterfly on the back of the tracing with paint that is a little deeper than the color of the butterfly so that it will show up well on the fabric. Always use a color that you know will show up on your fabric.

2. Stamp the outlined tracing on the fabric, pressing down with your fingers. Do this quickly before the paint on the tracing becomes dry and then remove it. Clean off tracing with tissue and mineral spirits in case you want to use it again.

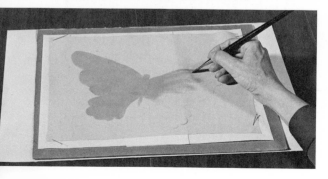

3. With a fairly large brush, mix on your palette yellow enamel, a little orange and yellow oil tube paint, and mineral spirits. Brush this thin mixture over the entire butterfly.

4. Mix yellow enamel, a little red enamel, and orange oil tube paint and brush on the veins in the wings and accent the scallops of the lower wings.

5. With the "heavy white" which you have already mixed, brush on the edges of the upper wings and add a spot on each wing.

6. With a pointed brush, mix red and green enamel to make brown, add a little orange oil tube paint and mineral spirits and paint the feelers. Accent the body, the scallops, and markings on lower wings.

Practice all of these steps on scraps of your fabric first.

The Stencil Method

To make a stencil, buy a paper called Vellum at any artists' supply store, as it is transparent.

This method can be used on any fabric, no matter what the color or thickness. Practice using a stencil on scraps of fabric first to learn the right consistency of the paint so that it will spread easily but not spread underneath the stencil. Mineral spirits should always be mixed in the paint on your palette, as the enamel right out of the can is too thick. Test it on scraps of your fabric to see how it spreads. Except in the case of painting on dark or brilliant-colored fabric, which is described at the end of this chapter, your first coat of paint is always a thin coat on which you later add shading and finishing touches. Try to avoid too many coats of paint, as it makes a stiff effect when dry.

Practice brushing on your first coat by starting *on* the stencil, allowing the brush to move from the stencil onto the fabric. This prevents the hairs of the brush from slipping under the stencil and spreading the paint beyond your cutout. Hold your stencil down tight to the fabric with your left hand.

The following step-by-step instructions on using a stencil to paint sea gulls was done with just one stencil for all the birds. However, if you want to paint a design, for instance, of a bunch of flowers with leaves around them, you will have to make more than one stencil; at least one for the flowers and another one for the leaves, because a stencil that has been cut leaving very thin spaces between the flowers and the leaves will make it difficult to keep the color of the flowers and the leaves from spreading into each other, so study your design and divide it into as many stencils as you think will make it easy. Start by painting the flower stencil first, removing it and then over it place the leaf stencil. If you want to add butterflies or birds to the design, make a separate stencil for them and you can place them on the tip of a leaf or anywhere you want in the design.

The following steps show how to use a stencil and the same procedure should be followed no matter what the design. Prepare your paints as explained in chapter 1.

1. Place a heavily outlined tracing of the sea gulls under your stencil paper and trace it through and with small scissors cut out the design on your stencil.

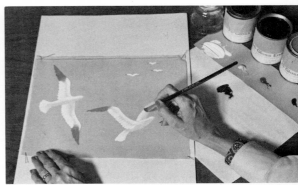

2. Place your fabric on a piece of white paper under which is a piece of cardboard and pin down the fabric at each corner. Then place the stencil on the fabric exactly where you have planned your design to be and pin down the stencil on the fabric to hold it in place. Mix white enamel on your palette with a little mineral spirits and proceed to brush a base coat on the body and wings. Add a little black enamel to the white enamel on your palette to make gray and brush on the tips of the wings.

3. Remove stencil and with a small brush smooth out any ragged edges on the sea gulls. Then, with the "heavy white," brush in the feathers one at a time by starting at the edge of the wings and brushing toward the middle of the wings, doing the same on the tails. Edge the top of the wings and body with "heavy white."

4. Mix black enamel with a little mineral spirits and with a small brush paint the tips of the wings right over the gray base coat by starting at the outer tips of the feathers and brushing toward the middle.

5. With black enamel and a pointed brush paint the eyes. Mix red and green enamel with a little yellow oil tube paint to make a light brown and paint the beaks and legs. With mineral spirits clean off your stencil in case you want to use it again. Remove paper from underneath your fabric and replace with a clean piece and let dry overnight.

Painting on Dark or Brilliant Fabric

Since paint soaks into fabric, it is necessary on dark or brilliant colors to build up a certain amount of paint on the surface to overcome the fabric color. Get your design on the fabric by using "heavy white" paint with a pointed brush freehand, using the stamped-on method, or by stencil.

In mixing whatever color you need for your subject, add "heavy white" to it and some mineral spirits, but not enough to make it thin, just so it spreads easily and does not completely soak in. Naturally, this will not be the desired final color you want, but it makes a base for it. Paint all parts of your design in this manner by including "heavy white" in each color you mix, unless there is black or some other dark color in some parts of the design. Then just brush it on as it is.

Next paint in your shading and final details. Practice painting on scraps of dark or brilliant fabric and try to keep from brushing on too much paint, as it will become very stiff when dry.

The following simplified step-by-step illustrations are of red poppies and green leaves on royal blue fabric.

1. With "heavy white" outline the back of the design, then turn it over and stamp on fabric.

2. Mix red enamel, orange oil tube paint, and "heavy white" and brush in the petals completely.

3. Mix green enamel, yellow oil tube paint, and "heavy white" and paint leaves and stems.

4. Mix red enamel and red oil tube paint and paint the dark shading on petals. Mix green enamel with a little black enamel and paint shading on leaves and stems.

Mix "heavy white" with yellow and orange oil tube paint and highlight edges of petals. With black enamel paint in the black centers and seeds. Remove paper underneath and replace with clean paper and allow to dry overnight.

Heavy White

"Heavy white" is mentioned many times throughout this book. It is a combination of white enamel and oil tube paint in approximately equal amounts, mixed together on your palette with a palette knife until very smooth. If it is correctly mixed, it will stay in a pile and not spread out. This combination of paints is one of the most important facets of painting on fabric that this book presents. Its value will become very apparent as you start painting. It is absolutely necessary in painting on dark or brilliant colors, highlighting a petal or a feather, and getting a smooth accented edge for a finished look.

In the accompanying photograph, the use of "heavy white" is shown and explained. Dark fabric was used to show it well; however, the subjects are not a finished product, but just show the use of "heavy white."

In the accompanying photograph, the use of "heavy white" is shown and explained. Dark fabric was used to show it well; however, the subjects are not a finished product, but just show the use of "heavy white."   1. This shows the use of "heavy white" by picking it up with your brush on one corner (left side), making a stroke that leaves a heavy edge on one side. Then by twisting your brush in your fingers to the right you can make a stroke that leaves a heavy edge on the other side. Practice doing this.   2. The petals of a daisy are shown in a front and side view using this technique.   3. The same effect is illustrated on a dogwood flower, accenting the petals and ridges in the petals.   4. By using "heavy white" with any color oil tube paint you want, this could be any colored rose. Mix the "heavy white" and oil tube paint on your palette, and by picking it up on one side of your brush you can control it to accent the petals.   5. The feathers on this sea gull were enlarged just to show the use of "heavy white." With this size bird, a number 8 flat sable brush was used. Pick up the "heavy white" on your palette and start at the outer edge of the feather, using your brush sideways. Press down on your brush and the paint will spread off on both sides of the brush. Practice doing this.   6. Mix green and yellow enamel with "heavy white," since this is on a dark fabric, and paint leaves. By adding "heavy white" and some yellow oil tube paint to the mixture, you can accent the highlights on the leaves.

Painting an Abstract

An abstract can be anything you want to create that is the reversal of traditional or representational art. The following instructions will show you how to paint an abstract by using masking tape. The tape comes in various widths and we shall use the ¾" width. By taking different lengths of the tape and sticking them on the fabric, you can make angles, squares or oblongs. Experiment with the tape until you arrive at something that pleases you. Paint the open areas in variations in tone or a combination of colors. The next day, after it has dried, pull off the tape, and the color of the fabric you have used will be a dominant part and should complement your original creation.

Don't hesitate to try this, as it requires no special art training, except practice mixing the enamels and mineral spirits and learning how to spread them on different fabrics. Use a large flat sable brush, like size 14 or 16, because a small brush requires many strokes to cover a big area and will cause streaking and overpainting. You should add mineral spirits to the paint at each step, as the enamel right out of the can is too thick to spread easily. Practice on scraps of fabric to test the mixture of paint and mineral spirits. In this type of painting, mix an extra amount of paint on your palette for each color, because if you run out of the color before you have finished, it is very difficult to remix that color to match what you used originally.

The following step-by-step instructions will show you how to do an abstract in tones of black, charcoal, gray and light gray on white fabric. Prepare your paints as described in chapter 1.

1. Take a piece of cardboard with a smooth piece of clean white paper on top, then place the fabric over it and pin down at each corner to the cardboard.

2. Stick various lengths of masking tape to the fabric to make the arrangement, making sure the ends of the tape make a sharp corner or clean-cut angle.

3. With your brush take black enamel right out of the can and mix it on your paper palette with mineral spirits so that it will spread easily. Paint in all the lower spaces.

4. With your brush add some white enamel and mineral spirits to the black enamel on your palette to make a charcoal color and fill in the upper three oblongs.

5. Add more white enamel and mineral spirits to the charcoal paint on your palette to make gray and paint all the upper spaces.

6. Add more white enamel and mineral spirits to the gray on your palette to make a very light gray and paint the last three spaces.

7. Let dry overnight then pull off the tape. The white of the fabric under the tape defines the arrangement, making a bold effect. The edges may not be perfectly straight, but this is unimportant.

3 Handpainted Fashions

Well-designed handpainted clothes have remained in good taste for many years. Like all other forms of fine handwork, handpainted fashions can be exciting to the wearer and give her a sense of having something special.

There are photographs of handpainted clothes and fashion accessories in this book to give you ideas of what it is possible to paint. However, don't hesitate to try your own original creations, as that is one of the purposes of this book—to inspire!

An important thing to consider when you are painting clothes is that the colors you use in your design are complementary to the color of the fabric and the placement of the design is flattering to the wearer. If you are creating a design for a dress, long or short, keep in mind that a painting that flows from the shoulder to the hem gives a long-line illusion and is flattering to any figure. Don't concentrate a design around the hips or the bust, as this tends to accentuate and widen these areas and has an undesirable effect.

In painting clothes for a small size consider that too much or too large a design can be overpowering to a small person, and the garment will dominate instead of enhance. Clothes in large sizes such as 16 or .18 should be treated specially. The best rule to follow is to have the design go up or down the middle or on one side as the eye will follow this long line.

The style and cut of a dress helps you determine the placement of designs; for instance, if it has panels, your design can accent the panels. Or, if it has pockets, painting something on the pockets can be effective. A yoke around the neck can be painted and is flattering to the face. Repeat at least some of your design on the back of any clothing. A woman wants to look interesting from the rear as well as from the front.

Don't feel confined to just flowers on clothes, even though they lend themselves beautifully to wearing apparel. There are many ideas especially for sportswear, such as sailboats on denim skirts and jackets, sea gulls on casual clothes, tropical and game fish, colorful birds, animals like tigers, leopards, cats, dogs, and monkeys. For the bridge fans you can paint playing cards on a jacket or a dress. For a backgammon devotee you can use some of the design on the board, the dice, cups, and the men for a very colorful and interesting effect. For tennis enthusiasts paint rackets and balls on blouses and jackets, and for golfers paint golf clubs, golf bags, and the numbered flags that are on the greens.

A pantsuit can be painted by having the design start at the bottom of the pants and continue up one leg or both. Then the design can start again at the bottom of the jacket and end up toward the neck. Paint some of the design on the back of the jacket and either the back of both legs or just one.

Nightgowns and robes can be very delicately painted, making them special for a gift. A touch of the design on fabric slippers can make a lovely ensemble. Housecoats and hostess gowns can be painted specially for someone by utilizing the decor of her home for the theme of the design. For instance, if the decor has an Oriental feeling, use motifs or flowers pertaining to this. Or if the theme is Early American, use bouquets of old-fashioned flowers. If the theme is contemporary, paint something bold in an abstract manner.

When creating a design for a fabric handbag, keep in mind that it should be wearable with many colored clothes. For instance, paint a summer bag with a combination of many pastel colors to go with any pastel-colored garment, or brilliant colors to go with dark or brilliant clothes. A handbag and a pair of fabric shoes can be painted to match (as illustrated).

A hat can be painted with colors to blend in with any clothing (as illustrated).

A solid color scarf which you can make yourself into a square or oblong can be effectively painted to tie in colorwise with any clothing.

Kitchen and hostess aprons can be decorated with all kinds of subjects, such as fruits, vegetables, chickens, birds, and so on.

Handpainted ties can be especially painted for men's casual and sportswear with such subjects as tennis, golf, baseball, basketball, skiing, and other sport motifs; however, floral and Oriental designs are acceptable.

You can monogram clothes, handbags, or any other item by getting a package of monograms that are used for embroidery in yard goods departments. These monograms are transferable on fabric by pressing. Use one initial at a time and press them on. On some surfaces, such as a handbag, use the stamped-on method described in chapter 5. Use the same technique of painting as any other subject. Put some shading or a darker line along one side of the initials to give them form. Practice doing this on scraps of fabric first. Monograms are not difficult, just tedious, and require a good pointed brush plus a steady hand. Design your own monogram by using your initials in script as you normally write them. Trace them in the size you need and use the stamping-on method.

Black satin dress with white dogwood.
G. G. Grimshaw

Black nylon blouse and crepe pants
with cheetah painted on one leg.
G. G. Grimshaw

Black and ivory crepe dress with white magnolias.
Navy brushed denim wraparound skirt with tiger.   *G. G. Grimshaw*

White nylon blouse with Siamese cat. *G. G. Grimshaw*

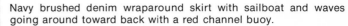

Navy brushed denim wraparound skirt with sailboat and waves going around toward back with a red channel buoy.

White jacket with nautical code flags.

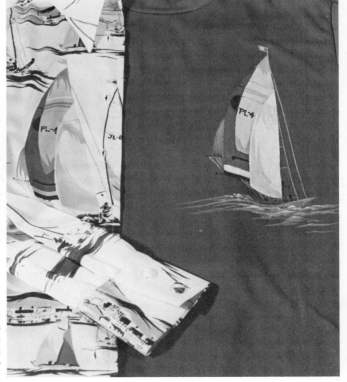

Navy nylon pullover with sailboat which was painted to match one of the sailboats on the printed blouse. Some of the design from any printed item can be painted on any accessory or clothing to make a coordinated effect.

White nylon umbrella with yellow and orange butterflies tipped with black.

Brown satin, black faille, and black peau de soie clutch bags with hummingbirds and flowers.

Black faille purse and shoes with white gardenia.

Blue acetate scarf with head in natural colors. *G. G. Grimshaw*

Pink acetate head scarf with multicolored butterfly. *L. Young*

White nylon T-shirt with stylized features. *G. G. Grimshaw*

Turtleneck nylon blouse with head. *G. G. Grimshaw*

Blue nylon half slip with daisies and forget-me-not design.

Pink nylon baby doll set with violets. *N. Mahr*

Red nylon T-shirt with black and white sea gulls.

Navy nylon T-shirt with green frogs.

Blue nylon T-shirt with white, yellow, and orange butterflies.

Kelly green T-shirt with tennis player in white dress and hat.

Beige nylon T-shirt with shocking pink, blue, and orange blocks.

Shocking pink T-shirt with monogram in white edged with red.

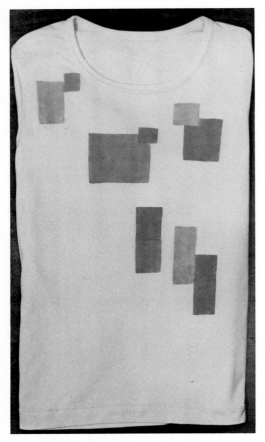

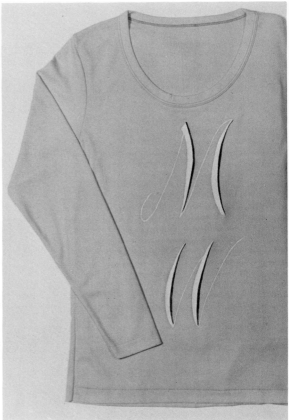

Man's T-shirt—for the man in your life.

Yellow nylon T-shirt with abstract design of aqua, blue, yellow orange, pink, red, and green.

Blue jeans with daisy design.

Navy T-shirt and blue jeans with red, yellow, and purple anemones.

Wicker Handbag. Panda bears were painted on a piece of felt which was glued on the bag and edged with gold braid. *N. Mahr*

Eyeglass and Cigarette Case. Long-stemmed roses are painted on silver cloth.

Blouse with brown monkeys hanging from branches on front and sleeve. *G. G. Grimshaw*

Blouse and Pants, painted down side of blouse and continuing on the leg with anchors, lifesavers, and rope. *G. G. Grimshaw*

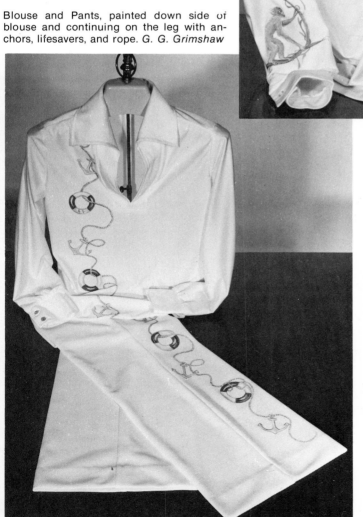

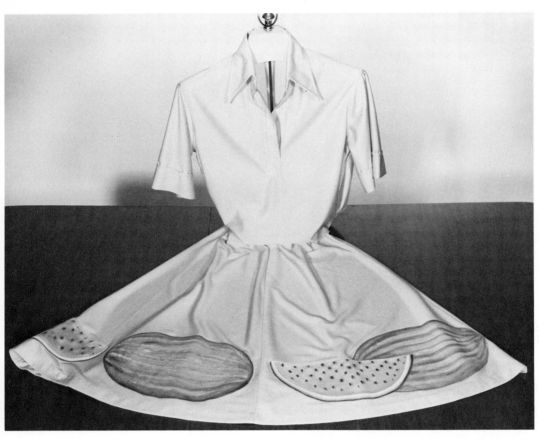

Blouse and Skirt, painted with watermelons going all around the bottom of the skirt. *G. G. Grimshaw*
Shell and Pants, painted with tulips going all around the bottom of both pieces. *G. G. Grimshaw*

Child's Playsuit, painted with toy soldier in bright red, blue, and black. *N. Mahr*

4 Handpainted Items for the Home

You can paint the cover of a pillow by removing the pillow first so that it will be flat. Flowers and birds can be painted to blend in with the color scheme of the room. Animal heads are effective in a man's room; cute dogs and cats can be fun for a child's room. Pillows for boats can be painted with nautical designs such as anchors, code flags, sea gulls, pelicans, and fish.

Wastebaskets: first paint the fabric with which you intend to cover the basket, then put glue around the top and bottom of the basket and stretch the fabric around it smoothly. You can cover the glued part with ribbon or braid. Suggested designs for kitchen baskets can be fruits and vegetables, garden variety flowers such as sunflowers, poppies, daisies, and cornflowers. For the living room the fabric can be more formal and the design more formal—birds with flowers or any design you think suitable for the room. Baskets can be covered with silk or satin for the bedroom, and the design should be complementary to the bedspread and the draperies. You can reproduce the design of the bedspread or the draperies on the basket. A basket can be monogrammed for the bathroom using colors in the bathroom.

Place mats, tablecloths, and luncheon sets paint beautifully with a variety of designs. If the table setting is formal, keep the design delicate and the colors soft. A portion of a design on your dishes can be reproduced on the cloth giving it a custom-made look. Informal and outdoor place mats can be of bright material, even stripes or checks, and painted with fruit like oranges, apples, and bananas, or tomatoes, little green onions, eggplant, carrots, and an ear of corn, making a very colorful design. Put a small part of the design on napkins. Be creative and use any subject you want, even something contemporary and modern.

Draperies and bedspreads are possible to paint by doing them in sections because you can paint at one time only as far as you can reach. Allow each section to dry overnight before continuing. Unless you can do your design freehand, it is best to use the stamped-on or stencil method and keep repeating the same design. Most drapery fabrics paint well except for an open weave. A bedspread can be beautiful with a large monogram in the middle using colors that are in the room. Flowers are always lovely on a bedspread—they can be very large and splashy or tiny and delicate.

Silk lampshades can be painted to match the design on the base or use the color of the base and create your own design. This should be complementary to the room. Don't let your paint be too thin, or it will soak through onto the lining underneath. This can be very tricky, so feel confident by having perfected your control of the paints before you try it.

Linen guest towels can be monogrammed or painted with a variety of subjects such as butterflies, fish, and flowers. Cocktail napkins can be attractive with roosters, an olive, a cherry, or a half slice of orange. Eyeglass cases give you an opportunity to create something very personal.

Ivory cotton and polyester apron with field flowers—poppies, daisies, cornflowers, and buttercups.

Blue striped denim apron with white daisies and
yellow butterfly.

Orange cotton apron with butterflies.

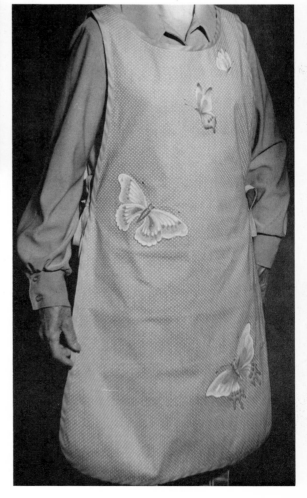

Burlap wall hanging with bamboo in shades of yellow, brown, and black. *G. G. Grimshaw*

Swan wall hanging, painted on heavy satin drapery material. *G. G. Grimshaw*

A piece of brilliant blue fabric painted with all white design using the stamped-on method. This idea of repeating the design can be used on many large items like draperies, bedspreads, and so on.

Wall hanging of mallard ducks with birch trees. *N. Mahr*

Grouping of vegetable pictures for the kitchen. *L. Young*

Grouping of fruit pictures for the kitchen or dining area, painted on fabric which was glued over paper prints that were already there. *N. Mahr*

Sheet and pillowcase, painted with long-stemmed yellow roses and buds.

White fringed linen cocktail napkins with brilliant colored roosters. *L. Young*

Green textured polyester place mat with peacock feather design. *G. G. Grimshaw*

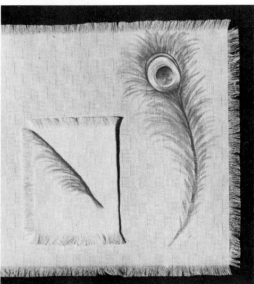

Lampshade on Japanese ginger jar base, painted with plum blossoms and birds.

Textured draperies, gold color and painted with white reeds and dragonflies.

Shoulder bag in canvas with monogram and purse accessories.

Pillows in silk and satin with irises, pansies, and roses. L. Young and G. G. Grimshaw

uest towels in Irish linen with butterfly, fish, bird and bamboo, and rose. N. Mahr

Blue jeans jacket and matching pants with field flowers.

Curtain in dotted swiss with pots of geraniums.

Luncheon set of Irish linen painted with magnolia and leaves.

Ties in polyester with contemporary heads and Japanese figure. G. G. Grimshaw

Wastebasket that was covered in canvas and
painted with Persian cat. G. G. Grimshaw

Wastebasket covered with suede cloth and painted
with leopard.

Tote bag in denim with
outline of white horses.

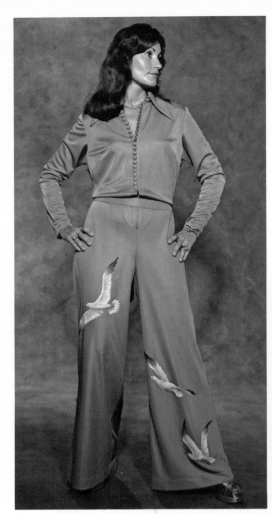

Jump suit in polyester with sea
gulls, which are also on back o
pants.

Wraparound skirt of brushe
denim with anemones goin
around to the back.

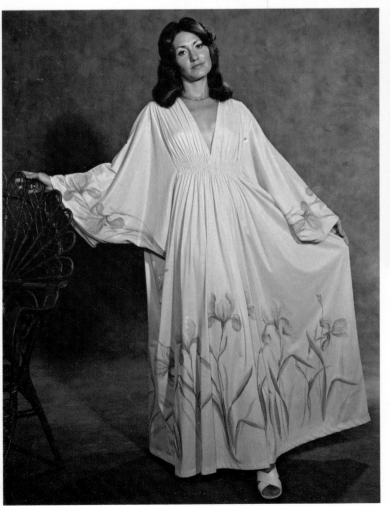

Caftan in Dacron and polyest
with iris painted on front, sleeve
and back.

Pantsuit in cotton with sea gulls, which also are on the back of the jacket and pants.

Pantsuit of Dacron and polyester with humming birds and hibiscus, also on back.

Pantsuit in Dacron and polyester with rose design front and back.

Wall hanging in drapery material with snowy owl. N. Mahr

Coat in ribbed silk with Japanese scene and figures.

Tablecloth in Irish linen with rose design. This tablecloth was painted twenty-five years ago. Some of the colors have softened, but the paint is still there.

Jacket of pantsuit in Dacron and polyester with dogwood on the front and back.

T−shirt in nylon with sea gulls.

Hat and blue jeans painted to match with field flowers.
L. Young

Blue jeans pants and vest painted with strawberri◀

5 Patterns

Sketches of most of the designs of the items photographed in this book are shown in this chapter to help you in painting them. The sketches can be identified by the accompanying descriptions.

Also, in this chapter a graph will be explained so that you can learn how to increase or decrease the size of these and other designs. This is very important to learn unless you can sketch and paint freehand.

Even though there is a large assortment of sketches and photographs in the book, your own desire for information on other subjects to paint can be satisfied in all public libraries, where books on every possible subject can be found. Most artists' supply stores carry books on a wide range of designs to interest the artist, including stencils for lettering.

Seed catalogs show photographs of flowers, fruit, vegetables, trees, and shrubs. They are important to have, as they show details that you will need to paint an authentic replica.

Wallpaper stores have remnants of paper with designs which can inspire you to paint them on something for your home. Many magazines have some of the finest artwork you can find. Don't copy another artist's painting, but let it inspire and give you ideas to create your own interpretation of the subject.

Greeting cards and other literature, especially those by the Metropolitan Museum and the Museum of Modern Art and other fine artist groups, have produced some of the best art you can find anywhere. These should inspire and help you, but not be copied.

Printed drapery fabric and chintz offer a wide variety of colorful designs that you can utilize and that can give you ideas.

As a suggestion, if you have the opportunity, take photographs of paintable subjects wherever you go—animals at the zoo, flowers in the parks, and birds in an aviary. They will be helpful to refer to when you decide to paint some of them.

When you get involved in painting, you will become more conscious and aware of things that attract and inspire you and you will find unlimited resources for ideas to paint.

Dogwood—which is a spray shown on the jacket of
a blue pantsuit in the color section.

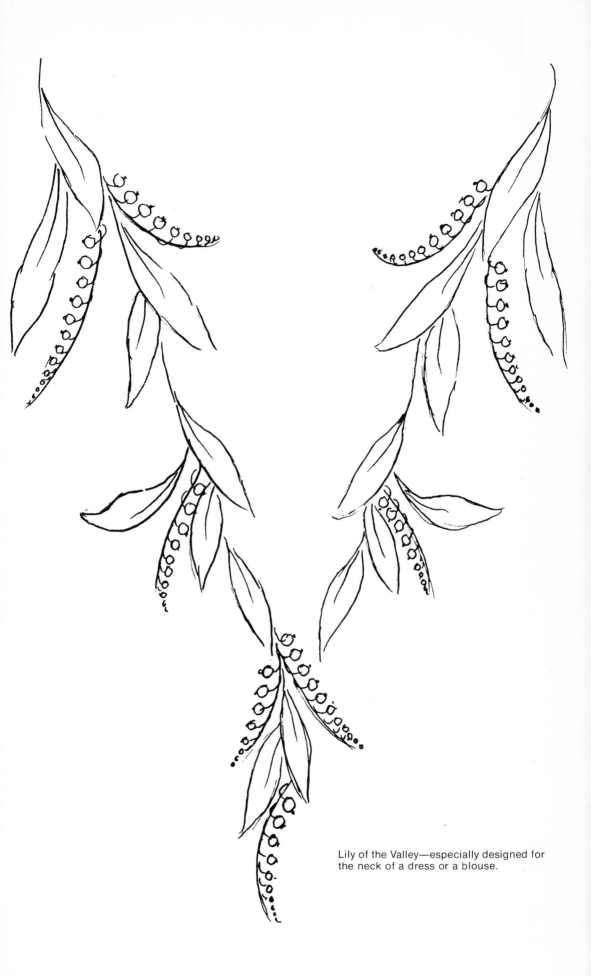

Lily of the Valley—especially designed for the neck of a dress or a blouse.

Goldfish—with undersea foliage.

Sea gulls—showing them at various angles in flight.

Horses—shown on a denim tote bag in the color section, painted using the stamping method and "heavy white."

Butterflies—that can be painted in various
colors with black wing tips.

Abstract—painted with a large brush in tones of
charcoal and gray. Black was used to accent.

Abstract—painted in black, charcoal, gray, and
pale gray. Instructions and illustrations of painting
this are shown in chapter 2 on Abstracts.

58

Fighting Cocks—can be very colorful with
red, green, and orange feathers.

Japanese Scene—with dancing figures and musician. Their clothing should be colorful and 0riental. The scene shows a scraggly pine and a plum tree with blossoms. Shown on a pink coat in the color section.

Field Flowers—a combination of poppies, daisies,
cornflowers, buttercups, and grasses, all in brilliant
colors, as shown on the jacket of a denim suit in the
color section.

Iris—as shown on the caftan in the color section, in
tones of purple, lavender, and blues with touches of
pink.

Pansies—are in brilliant colors, plus white and
yellow. These are shown on a pillow in the color
section.

Snowy Owl. This is a sketch of a snowy owl shown on a wall hanging in the color section. It was painted from a photograph in a book from the public library. Transparent Vellum paper, available in most artist supply stores, was used to make the stencil. A heavily outlined enlarged drawing was made of the owl to fit the size of the wall hanging. The drawing shows the eyes, beak, dark prominent feathers, and wooden piles. This was traced through onto the stencil paper and the whole owl—eyes, beak, and dark feathers—was cut out, leaving the wooden piles until later.

Pin down on your fabric the stencil which has had the owl cut out and paint in the whole owl with white enamel, "heavy white," and a little mineral spirits.

Remove the outer stencil and place the cutout owl, which has had the eyes, beak, and dark feathers in wings cut out, too, right over the painted owl. Mix yellow enamel and yellow oil tube paint and fill in the eyes. With black enamel paint the round pupil in the center of the eyes, the beak, and the dark feathers.

Remove the stencil and mix black and white enamel to make gray, then paint in shading and the lighter feathers on the body.

Cut out the wooden piles from your original stencil and place under the owl. Paint with gray and streak with black. *N. Mahr*

Persian Cat. These cats vary in color, but are most distinctive for their long fur. This white Persian cat is shown on a wastebasket in the color section.

Panda "Bears"—are black and white with definite black markings around the eyes. The head and back are white and the rest of the body is black, including the ears. They were painted from photographs in the *National Geographic Magazine*.

Monogram—shown on a T-shirt in black and white. You can create your own monogram by enlarging the initials of your own name in longhand, and by using the stamping-on method you can apply them on anything. Artist supply stores carry initials on stencil paper. Pattern departments in the yard goods section of stores have initials in many styles to iron on fabric for embroidery, but they can just as easily be painted.

ABCDEF
GHIJKL
MNOPQ
RSTUU
WXYZ

Alphabet—in a special script that can be enlarged,
using a graph explained in this chapter.

ABCDEFG
HIJKLMN
OPQRSTU
VWXYZ

Alphabet—in an elongated block style, that can
also be enlarged using a graph.

Anemone. This is a stylized version shown on a brushed denim wraparound skirt and on denim pants and T-shirt in the color section. Their colors are always brilliant.

Wall Hanging—a scene of mallard ducks, birch trees, and a stream and reeds.

Buttercups—a round five-petaled bright
yellow flower with an orange and brown
center. Included in the field flower
designs.

Rooster—very brilliant red comb, yellow
ruff, and green tail feathers. Painted on
cocktail napkins in chapter 4.

Hummingbirds—are the smallest of birds, with a very long beak, and are varied in color. Those photographed are ruby-throated with greenish bronze wings.

Cornflowers—a very special bright blue with a purple center. Their petals are very ragged. They are included in the field flowers on the denim jacket in the color section.

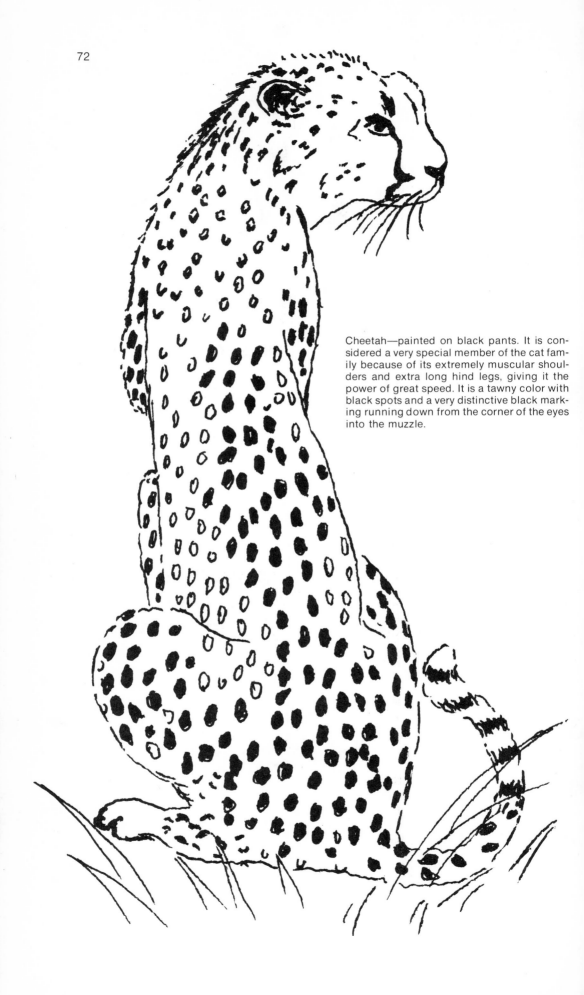

Cheetah—painted on black pants. It is considered a very special member of the cat family because of its extremely muscular shoulders and extra long hind legs, giving it the power of great speed. It is a tawny color with black spots and a very distinctive black marking running down from the corner of the eyes into the muzzle.

Leopard. One of the cat family; has a yellow, orange, and brown coat with very dominant black spots, a white muzzle, and underbelly. It is shown on a wastebasket in the color section.

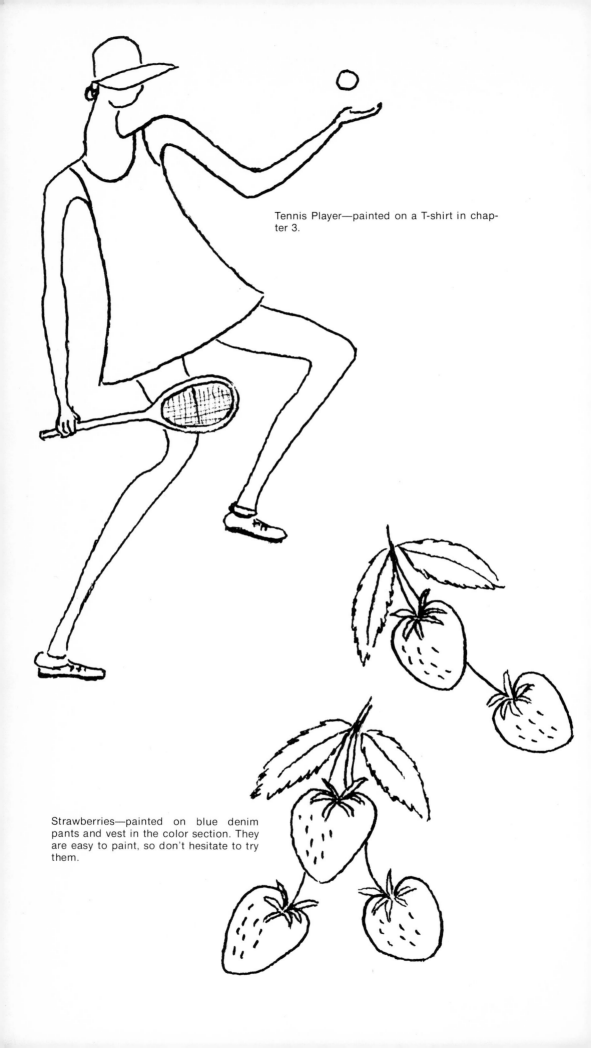

Tennis Player—painted on a T-shirt in chapter 3.

Strawberries—painted on blue denim pants and vest in the color section. They are easy to paint, so don't hesitate to try them.

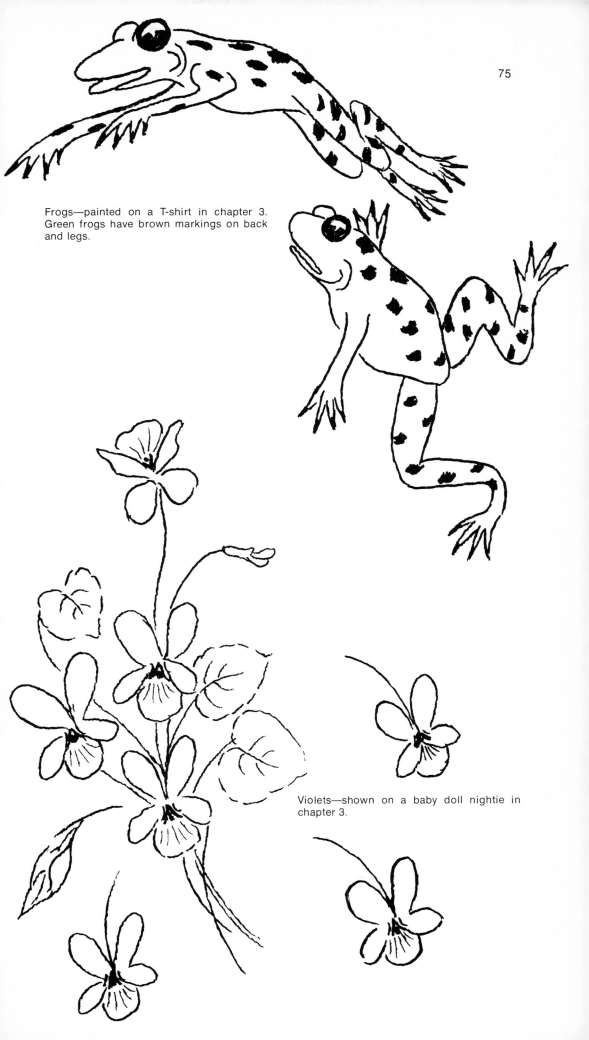

Frogs—painted on a T-shirt in chapter 3. Green frogs have brown markings on back and legs.

Violets—shown on a baby doll nightie in chapter 3.

Magnolia and Leaves—shown on a gray luncheon
set in the color section. It is a pure white flower with
extremely beautiful leaves, ranging from bright and
dark green leaves to brown as they age.

Roses—painted on a pillow and a pantsuit in the color section. One of the most beautiful of flowers, but difficult to paint. An artist once said: "Don't paint a rose so that if a petal fell it would make a thud!"

Nautical Code Flags—are shown painted around the bottom of a jacket in a black and white photograph. Each flag represents a letter of the alphabet or a word signal in brilliant colors of red, blue, yellow, black, and white. Stores carrying boating equipment can provide you with literature on code flags and other nautical signals such as buoys and so on.

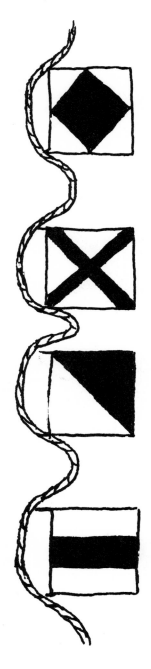

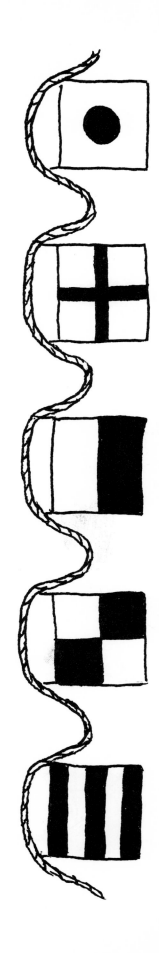

Daisies—painted all around the bottom of denim pants and T-shirt. Easy to do—try it!

Bamboo—painted on a burlap wall hanging in
shades of yellow, brown, and green.

Swans—on a wall hanging made from a leftover piece of pale blue drapery material. This was hung in a bedroom having the same colored draperies. The swans were painted from photographs taken in Portugal, where in their natural habitat many different views of them were possible. They have been a source of many oil paintings by *G. G. Grimshaw.*

Pots of Geranium—painted on a dotted swiss kitchen curtain in the color section. They are clay pots with very red geranium and buds; their leaves are distinctive—scalloped in green with dark markings.

Peacock Feather—has a brilliant blue green center with turquoise surrounding it and with gold and brown outlining it. The extending feathers are a green bronze. Each feather varies slightly and has an overall gold shimmer.

Siamese Cat—is a pale warm beige color with very dark brown and black markings on the face and legs and darker fur on the back and tail as it gets older. It is shown painted on a blouse.

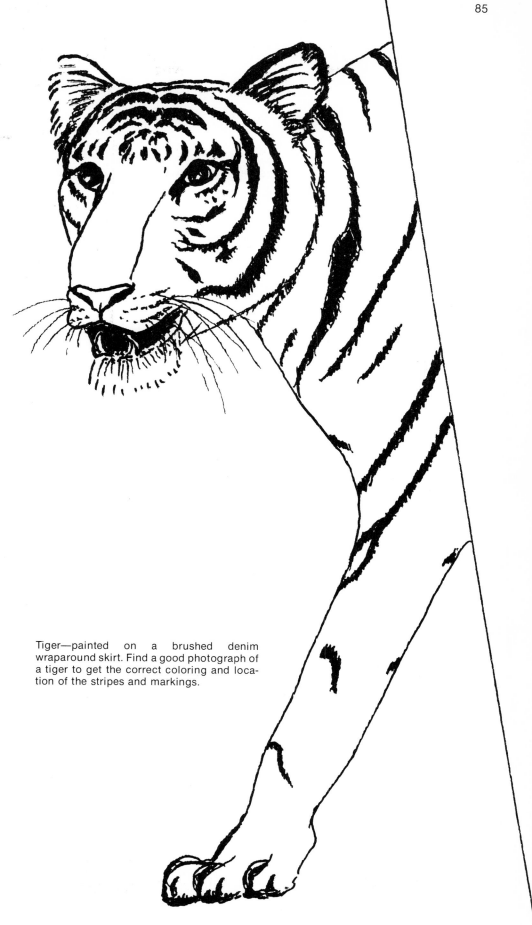

Tiger—painted on a brushed denim wraparound skirt. Find a good photograph of a tiger to get the correct coloring and location of the stripes and markings.

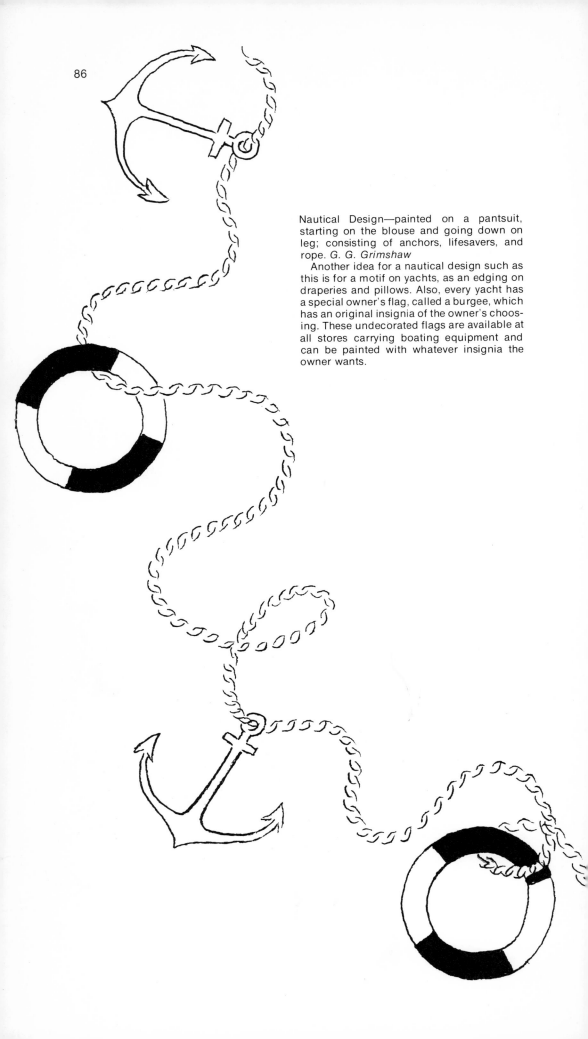

Nautical Design—painted on a pantsuit, starting on the blouse and going down on leg; consisting of anchors, lifesavers, and rope. *G. G. Grimshaw*

Another idea for a nautical design such as this is for a motif on yachts, as an edging on draperies and pillows. Also, every yacht has a special owner's flag, called a burgee, which has an original insignia of the owner's choosing. These undecorated flags are available at all stores carrying boating equipment and can be painted with whatever insignia the owner wants.

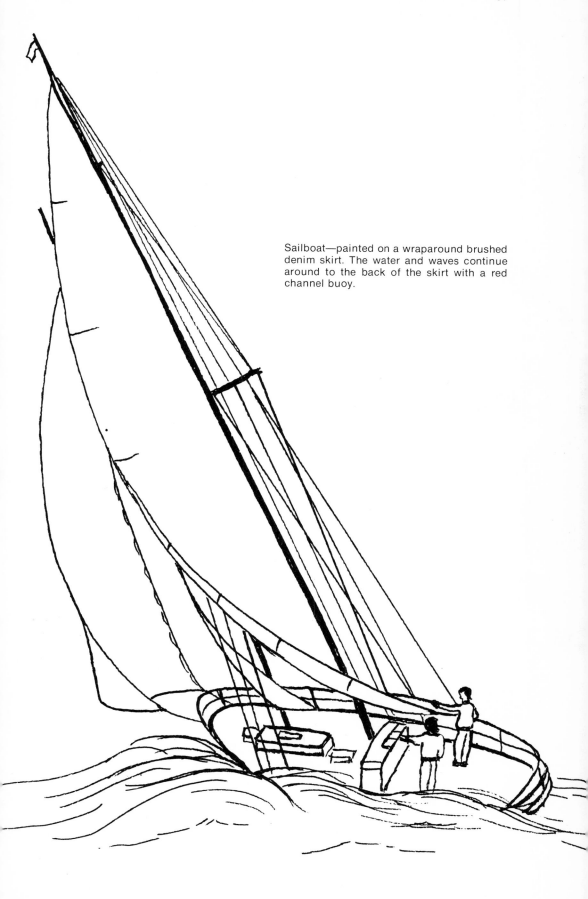

Sailboat—painted on a wraparound brushed denim skirt. The water and waves continue around to the back of the skirt with a red channel buoy.

Vegetables—are shown on a grouping of pictures in their natural colors. The individual vegetables were painted from the pictures on packages of seeds found in the market. Peas, peppers, tomatoes, carrots, corn, and radishes were painted on textured fabric which was placed over heavy cardboard and glued on the back. They were edged with colored sticky tape.

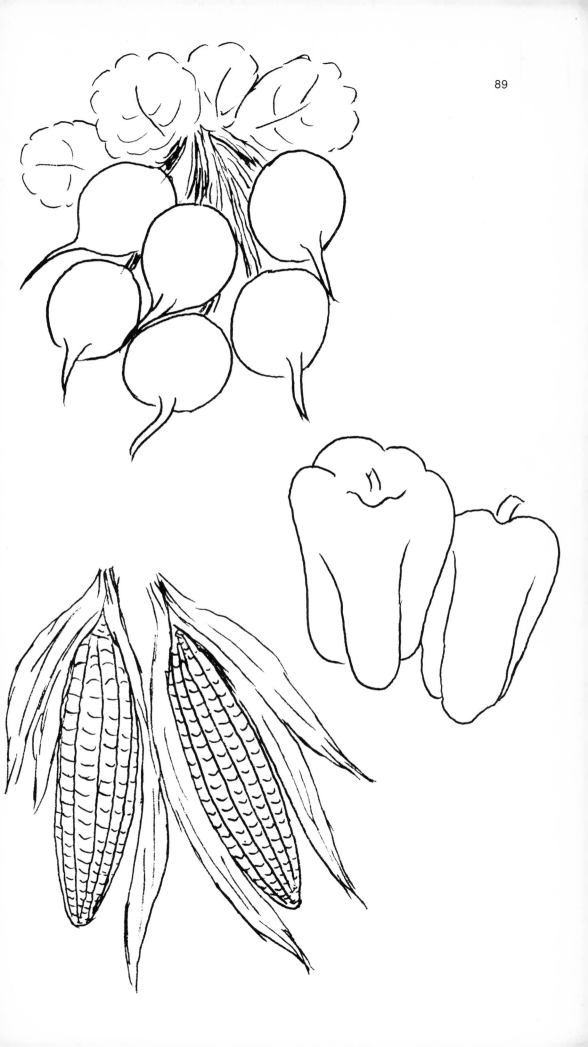

Enlarging or Decreasing Size of Design

One way to increase the size of a design is by using graph paper, as this illustration will show. Transparent Vellum graph paper is available in most office supply stores where they carry architectural equipment. This paper is divided into squares varying in size.

By using transparent graph paper, you can trace your design onto it without having to square off the original copy of your design.

If you are planning to enlarge your design, decide how much larger you want it for the size of the object you are painting. In the illustration of ivy leaves which has been enlarged ½", the graph paper which was used was divided first into small ⅛" squares and also divided with heavier lines into 1" squares. All graph paper is ruled off in this manner, except the size of the small squares and the size of the large squares vary. There is a selection of sizes from which to choose according to your needs. If the size of the paper is not large enough for your design, it can be taped together.

After you have traced your design on the graph paper that has 1" squares, use the following instructions to increase the size of the ivy leaves.

With another piece of graph paper which is exactly the same as that which you used originally, draw 1½" squares with a ruler and pencil right over the squares that are there, making them heavy enough for you to see.

Then start at the top stems of the ivy leaves and draw them with pencil in the comparable square to your original copy. Draw from one small square to another and keep checking to see if your drawing is at the same point in the increased 1½" squares as in the 1" squares of your original. Continue to enlarge each leaf and lengthen each stem one at a time until you have reached the bottom.

Have an eraser handy, as it can be frustrating when trying this for the first time, but after having enlarged the first leaf you will know just what to do.

If you want to decrease the size of your design, the same procedure is reversed. Instead of increasing the size of the squares, decrease them with ruler and pencil to ¾" or ½" squares on another piece of graph paper.

As stated previously, graph paper is available in various size rulings, or grids, to suit your needs. You can use these, but it is instructive to know that you can increase or decrease the size of the squares yourself if necessary.

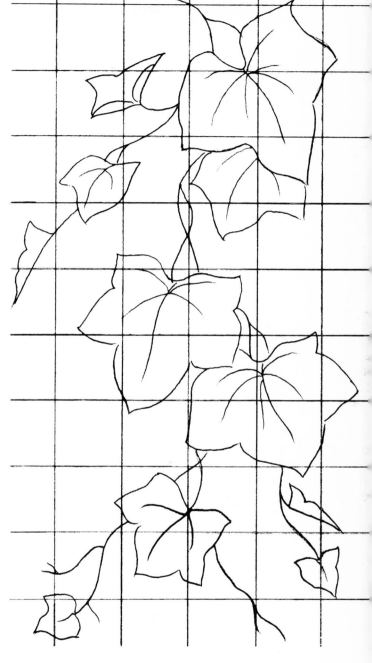

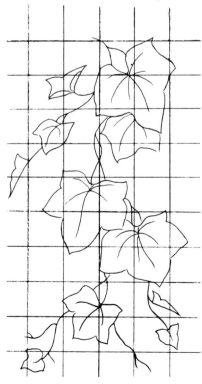

Here is an example of enlarging a design of ivy leaves by squaring off the original design or using graph paper, which is already squared. Then with a piece of larger squared paper, start at the top stems and leaves and draw from one block to another, making them comparable to the stems and leaves on the smaller squared graph.

6 Helpful Facts

The oil tube paints you squeeze out on the foil paper will remain usable for many days. Some oil tube paints have an excess of oil in them that squirts out when squeezed. When this happens, put it on an absorbent piece of paper for a little while until the oil drains off. The enamel and oil tube paints you have mixed on your palette will dry very quickly and cannot be saved for the next day's painting.

When you have finished your painting, cover the "heavy white" on your palette with a piece of Saran Wrap and it will remain usable for days.

The mineral spirits in your glass jar can be used again by letting it settle overnight. Pour off the clear spirits the next day.

Take good care of your brushes by cleaning them thoroughly in the mineral spirits *as soon as* you are through using them. Never put them down without cleaning them. If the enamel is left to dry on them, it will cause the hairs to spread and your brushes are ruined. Facial tissues are good for cleaning brushes.

Regular notebook and typing paper are suggested for use as palettes because they have a slick surface and are inexpensive. When your palette gets too full of paint, just put a clean piece of paper on top of it.

Shake the cans of enamel well before you first open them, then always stir again each time used. When the enamel is first opened it will require a small amount of mineral spirits when you are thinning it on your palette, but it tends to thicken in time and will require more mineral spirits. When you have finished painting, replace the lids on the cans tightly by placing a piece of facial tissue over the lids and stepping on them. A little film may form on the top of the paint overnight. This should be removed so that you can dip in easily.

Everyone makes mistakes and drops or smears paint on their fabric. To remove, place a piece of folded facial tissue underneath the spot and with a clean rag, which has been dipped in clean mineral spirits, rub the spot until paint comes off. Remember that the mineral spirits spreads very quickly through the fabric, so don't let it spread into your design if the spot is close to it. If the dropped paint cannot be removed entirely, add more design after you have allowed the area to dry.

Try to complete your painting in less than three or four hours as your base coat of paint, being thin, dries and makes blending and shading difficult; however, some details such as fine lines, small dots, or a deep concentration of color in a small area may be added after it is dry. Avoid overpainting any large area.

After you have finished painting, remove pins and carefully lift the fabric and remove the paper from underneath in case the paint soaked through. Replace it with a clean piece of paper to let dry. On some thick fabrics the paint will not soak through onto the paper, but don't take a chance; always put a piece of cardboard and then a piece of paper underneath. There is no further treatment to make it washable and dry-cleanable.

Your painting should dry overnight, but if the weather is particularly damp and cold, it may take a little longer. If after twenty-four hours your design has not dried, it will be because you had too much oil tube paint in your mixture of paints and not enough enamel. The oil tube paints are added strictly for color, and there should always be at least a half-and-half combination. Don't try to dry your painted fabric in any way other than just the normal overnight airing.

If you are painting on a blouse or any other clothing, put the cardboard with paper on top in between the front and the back so that your paint won't soak through to the other side. After painting, carefully remove pins and lift fabric to remove paper underneath, leaving the cardboard. Then a hanger can be slipped into the garment from the bottom. Remove cardboard as you are hanging it up to dry. Let the front of any clothing dry completely before attempting to paint on the back.

Learn to pick up your paint with your flat brushes so that you have control of the paint when you brush it on the fabric. You can do this by mixing the paint you want on your palette, wiping off most of the paint with facial tissue, then with a sliding motion pick up the paint on one side of the brush so that the paint is concentrated in one corner of the brush. You can then control this paint and make a very small dot or a sweeping stroke like the stem for a flower. Also you can make a shaded stroke by having a light color on your brush and then pick up on one corner a darker tone of the same color. The result is a stroke of paint shaded from light to dark.

After mixing paint on your palette with your brush, get in the habit of wiping off the brush with facial tissue so that it is not full of paint. Then with your brush you can pick up your paint on the palette with a flat stroke and have control of it.

When using your pointed brush, dip it in the paint you are using on the palette and, by holding it fairly level and twirling it, all the hairs will come to a point. This makes it possible to paint fine lines, tiny dots, and small details.

If it is possible, have your paints, palette, brushes, and so on, on a separate table next to your right side unless you are left-handed. Also, a tilted table like a drawing board is desirable to paint on, as then your vision is correct.

Index